Also by Stuart McPherson

Waterbearer (Broken Sleep Books, 2021)

Pale Mnemonic (Legitimate Snack, 2021)

OBLIGATE CARNIVORE

McPherson

ISBN: 978-1-915079-33-6

The author has asserted their right to be identified as the author of this Work in accordance with the Copyright, Designs and Patents Act 1988

Cover designed by Aaron Kent

Edited and typeset by Aaron Kent

Broken Sleep Books Ltd
Rhydwen,
Talgarreg,
SA44 4HB
Wales

Contents

I.

II.

III.

IV.

Obligate Carnivore

Stuart McPherson

I.

Hit the age of reason with a stick. Feel it swell, a humpback bridge. Over water spilt on instructions and *abridged*. Mistaking Rorschach then, for the silhouette of man mismatched: the carcass of a horse. A boy skipping stones into a mothers mouth who spits them back. Remorse for a dawn that never arrives. Its father zipped away in the blackness of a bag strikes the age of reason with a belt. Starved of food, prods its pink belly-bloat. A waxing moon begins to lift, impales a boar that squeals. Bleeds testosterone. Suddenly becomes a suckling pig.

Everyday Haunting Practice

You, as the turning page
Every breath of air drawn in

Idle gaps, the three of swords slid across
Flipped over with a snap

A pigeon egg beneath the damson tree
Returning there, the bird

To cats clawing slim trunks
To empty sticks, the ghosts of feathers

And you, within the pocket lint
Entropy, or the linear movements

Of every house we've ever slept in
Our auras leeching into walls, the corners of

your face, etched, in the bluest
Of distant light

Buried Boys Always Come Back

The buried boy beneath my heels
returns with a scalpel
How is he complete, *Achilles*?

When unable to talk about
anything but ligaments
The fibula, the calcaneus

And his mouth full of leaves
Maybe figments left over
All fallen off

Or purposefully pushed in
To the top and bottom of the frenum
Ankles cut at forty-five degrees

Voice like October he appears
Can't talk about Ouija, *bad luck*
or the current consequences of

For those with cracked fingers
Trodden on and bruised, at the nail-
bed, at our knuckles

Swinging the Fire Axe

Your weight is heavy in the hand. Your handle is anti-slip.
Lipless face steeled and flat, stood angled.

In the cutting chair propped, not suited to play. Airwaves
maybe; *afternoon cricket.*

To work solo slowly on the road. Found featherless, dead
pheasant.

Unable to climb stairs. Push an axe-head beneath sheets,
tuck a young boy in, not leaning towards unpleasant ends.

To swing you back father, to split between the lines. A sharp
pointed pick, a punctured fontanelle.

As emptied hearts quickly darken, are embezzled. Quite
possibly blinded.

Fantasy Beast

Father manifests in shapes.
Triangles, squares.
A familiar set of clothes
worn away.

Words behind lips.
A circle of index fingers and
thumbs dipped in soap bubbling
out like a long sock.

Father chopped from a tree.
Lit up with a finger click that
nobody sees or feels the gradient
of its warmth.

The chime of flint.
Struck as melancholic song as
we ride out with horsemen
towards death.

Too heavy for itself.
As soil exhumes in the fire.
The voice a threaded screw
coughing rust.

Expressionless.
Licking wounds, a dry tongue
on the subsidence knocked from
father's shoulders.

Shovelled into piles and mixed.
With the water and lime
mortared between bricks, ill-
fitted, angular.

Foundations or a cage.
A tower to stand atop swaying.
Edges crimped right up to
the toes.

It's better just to prop up, fulcrum.

Mute the heart-shaped stones.
The rattling behind your eyes.
Father, disguised as Minotaur, or
some other fantasy beast.

Broken Chair

I smash a chair   a bent frame swung not in rage   but
relent

To see it gape   my face a wet cloth wringing gaps

and holding our gaze, *the chair*, we pause   how quiet and still
the air   his pointing fingers bruise bones

We stood   in syrup light   unable to form the
consonants or vowels other than those

pushed from our father's mouths   we stretch out the
awkwardness in our calves

and walk, chew on everything   reveal the chair
its splinters   its dowels sharpening in our pockets

We practice vowels, repeal verbiage   and it's strange that
throughout the years

I've seen him yield so much more   than I *ever* have, or
navigated,   such   angry   major   arcs

House Spider on Curtains
(I.M Sarah Kane)

Trapped under every evening
The jagged way it runs
Mother and son mouths rounded like coal

Lullabies so gently sung as eyes are
caught eightfold before sleep
Recurring dreams of inexact families

The separate parts, mandibles, abdomens
Silk around my legs strung up and bunched
Like *Calla Lilies* in bloom for the hypnagogic

Those frozen at four forty-eight a.m.
Folded joints to hair tips hooked into walls
and dropped below window frames to places

The willows weeping by a river where I meet
myself walking backwards ~ the language
The pollen rising up from the casing of
a pillow

My Mothers Second Death, Resurrected

A call will come to tell me that
you sleep, that it's time for me
to rest, but now

A new Halloween
Undressed
And leading brightly out

To copper scales on concrete
Last breaths
A success I needed you to see

Perhaps, the success of *me* instead
And so they starved
Scissoring the questions then

Of air and riverbeds, old rocks
and weed or crescent dirt
My fingernail a broken moon

Hanging on this strangest hope
Of seeing your possessions
sifting in a pan

Drop yellowness
Tilted sadly on a fools head
In procession, as angular as Gold

For Shapeshifters

I learnt about love the same way a boy learns to slide down the
prongs of a snake

The sistrum   In the burrows where we lay together, blue
buttoned   An examination

of venom   How its point slices open with every flick
every odor on the nerve   a knife

If you find me slithering on my stomach   sit me in the shade
beneath the rungs

This shape   To be serpentine

For at the top of the ladder you'll find my *other* body   not this
grave   this mausoleum redesigned   and forever desecrated

A Skull in the High Tide of Masculinity

Screens define schematic doctrines of touch
our intimacy as process / lean six sigma sex
a synaesthesia of obliques / these glistening
abdominals attached to analogue VHS / a sleaze
kneading of breasts / underfed with cheap physics
the formality of mechanized thrusts / repetitive
equations for scratching / the back of my
occipital crest / learning to be fed
tapes spooling in the tray / these famished young
men / fan flames / of malnourishment / of frailty
our mainstay / the way we *swarm* / the way

> we *fascinate*
> these lullabies
> so gently / sung
> like trepanning
> or how / we might
> learn / to smash
> our own skulls

When You Leave Me, I Will Howl

Darkness pins us to the circle from nose to ribs. How to teach about difference. Tails between legs and claws? If I'd have had a son, I'd file down his teeth. Use his black liquid to write eulogies on the rocks. Maybe, from faraway, the lost will write back. I've fed you, warmed you, caught lean meat. The ice-melt on your tongue fresh from cradling fish. We've howled but you haven't seen what I've seen, and there is much worse yet to come young daughter, sleeping soundly beneath a lid, this sparkling convex quilt.

Dog Tail In Scissors

Snipped off in haste without ceremony, and cut,
by those who boomerang separation into the arms
of sons. To observe the hang of sulphurous

lights, the restless bodies in sleep. Black mass at
the altar of the hidden. A bull clouding in his own
breath, the shrouded guilt of a matador.

Work hard proud admiral, to die in-chrysalis.
Know right from wrong but the sting of a bloody
stump.

Raising children with love as tails in a box drum
up against its lid. Deceive the dog nagging at the
gate before leaning towards

carnivorous intent. Kill pigs, cook bacon, fillet
steak. Young teeth bite down, meditate intensely
on pugilism.

Become terrified of noise; stray bullets, burst
balloons. That nostalgia is memory broken over
backs, and boyhood, as the vaguest of failed states.

Hunger

A memory of salt lick / of acid tang / a plate wrung from a
hand / *just give it to me*

Young limbs underfed / sipping puree from a spoon / sorry
baby brother / *for I must eat*

Apple sauce on pork / on poverty lines / rescinded dietetics
the calcium content of milk

An erasure of lists / mineral density / as divination / as
astrology / an empty table is dislocation / a shoulder slotting
in

Its folded wings / a paper crane / dampens hunger / stands
upright like a spear / in the lake / of *my old self*

And origami / is a learnt skill

Its methodologies can be sharpened / on the stones / still
resting / at the bottom / of our stomachs

Charcuterie

My assessment
begins by cutting
questions

into the
flesh of
assorted meats

Not digestible
but rather
the taste and

smell of
something
sentient

I sew the
slices with
thread

pierce them
with a stick to
form

something
two legged
A creature

that
makes sense
not by

running
wildly around
howling

or
fucking
things up

A concertina
of rotting cells
strung together

                  to form a
                  movement
                  of arms

and breath
An evolution
The hunt for

                  something more
                  substantial felt
                  deeply in the

marrow
Not the
songs

                  of men too
                  lost to string
                  together

a triumphant
chorus of
waypoints

                  or escape the
                  machine that tumbles
                  loose boiled skin

Aperture

It's *your* lens that I'm pushed through
A white flatness manta-raying in liquid
Held atop by tongs, shaken loose drops
More than latent under red light

If you'd have framed me by the lilacs
Not the ledge of your ragged outcrop
I wouldn't now be flooded,
like a bright ghost from the edges of film

II.

Self-Esteem Calendar

13 months in a year is bad luck

The summer was blown glass pinched across a mornings neck.
A   potential   of   orange   light   laced   with   ice,   lemon.
Short lived as sunsets, or parts of the body weakened by falling.
Its fractured ankles were oblique   and painfully displaced.

The heat when it broke
        Buddleia twisted upwards   Elkhorns dipped in
violet stooped above a hosepipe kink

                                    A butterfly

An accent smeared across the late afternoon

                Unable to wrap it around my arm the
way he wanted.   An imperfect figure eight,
                        forever looped

You were equidistant to the curve
A circle of birthdays or a sprung saddle ~ an
invisibility spell
Not late, just somewhere else you'd rather be
We played party games   *pass the parcel*

The calendar of my youth creased gently
                              in-between each sheet

A hand in Novembers
Under bedspreads
Three bodies
Two older than the other
On the lines of Apolis
Where it held its scent
The remnants of a harbour
or the afterword; its gutters
Curled around the edges
A face between legs
and caught
Amongst words vented
in false surprise
and sickening by
the bedside, small palms
A hint of curdled milk
The pretense of rescue attempts
always coming to nothing

On December twenty fifth
Glue latex to a cheek
Apply blood with fingers
Run and sit beneath the
tryptophan tree and let
vampire teeth cut the
corners of your mouth
A boy though, or a warning
Just slightly less alive than

There are questions I want to ask about illusions. How bedsprings feel on your back. About the instruments used to prise yourself away ~ a claw hammer, an oyster knife. I want to ask about the seasons and if you pressed your eye to the lens. Lined up my winter cheeks, my summer shorts. What about black pearls? How the shucker pierced your mantle. You're closer to the sea now and twisted inside a bottleneck. A potion, bats ears, poison ivy. The one that turns people into smoke. I think about the space you fill between walls and furniture, between months. I wonder if you knew ~ *your daughter died*. That the rest of us were mangled, run over, struck by lightning.

A faintness
of rubber   and blood
         The tread   filled
                   with Yellows Reds

Brittle white   My questions
         a hole   grated cleanly
                   in temporal

plates as
I wonder   Do you
         even   remember
                   me?

My spring math's problem is a misshapen set of seeds. A dandelion growing in a blown balloon, encased. Impenetrable as amber, as drilled mosquitos. To sample DNA is absent lucidity. How roots eventually find water; a discarded tuber can fill a room. Its ugly green leaves, white pinpricked petals.

Hold
me in your
hands. Comfort me
with talk of freedom
The sinew of decision
hanging from your teeth

Bad wolf
in a madness
of lengthening grass
Smeared crimson breaths
A discarded rotting carcass
The annihilation of a pack

I will
continue
to accelerate
until all of this fuel,
this body, has been extinguished

         Your fist leads a bicep
Leads the tendons in your neck
Mountainous

The stretch of skin tarpaulined across the
well of you; amorphous
         Your teeth within my daughters arm
and mine

             I float upon your waters
                your depths

She bathes me in the licorice
The root of all our discontent

I crack my knuckles
      The clicking in my jaw- *vibrato*
           Collecting remnants as I chew

In the house, April held him

"Stop crying or I'll make it so you never want to come back"

April was unexpectedly cold for that
time of year,

still occluded / February snow

October sat outside

"Stop crying or I'll make it so you never want to come back"

October was unexpectedly cold for
that time of year

October never held anyone

I don't remember the month
The windows were covered in
wings, *and* the walls

It's discourteous to lie to your
mother, I remember them hurting
as they fell

The earthworms, food for
a snake and foaming
on the curtains

To give semblance to truth
Explain the hydraulics of long
bodies crawling through rings

Like scars as the god of war
rained down, and I lied to
dry myself off

What is a calendar?
Other than self-realisation
condensed backwards
into paper

III.

Wolves at Distance

Voices in the oak trees, the dribbling brook.
Widening arms a wingspan. A vice holding
onto limp bodies drawn upwards by the
masseter, the pterygoids.

The crown of that church lipped as a tabletop.
Two scattered barrels shortened by a blade
and the memories of a sister stooped lonely on
its grounds beneath a fractured steeple, a roof.

A cranefly muted by a nearby howl. Its fragile
leg twitched on a palm and whispers tumbling
through the ryegrass. The hollowness a sphere
brushed against a gradual skin.

Roughened sisal rope burning though the
crease. Weeping bark notched; pitch sticky.
Of all the swinging weight. Botched daylight
bares sickle teeth, O slow yellow crescent.

Abattoir

We shared out our sleep.
The wind cupped us in its
hands, with taillights.

The callouses of men
twisting up the creel
and crudely stacked.

Pelts of animals once kept
between stonewalls and a
pale white whalebone are

soaking in the cold. Their
glass eyes, glass breath.
Our seat among them as

we rest, unbeknownst.
An intruder on the stairs,
a skinner knife in the draw.

The blotting of the sea a
blanket creeping up the
legs of a shivering child.

Plea Bargaining

I

Maybe they thought I was a girl, the judiciary. Maybe *he* did.
The rest were girls. Do the girls still think they're girls? They'll
be women now. I've never met any of them. I know I'm not a
boy, or a man, *I think,* after this.

II

Four hundred crooked pines. The kind with bent trunks
found in West Pomerania. That on rare occasion the desert
makes blood by thickening in the rain. Pours it from a gaping
jug neck to redden the family patch.

III

Why lenticular clouds oddly positioned look like throbbing.
That the underbelly of mammatus laments. The sacrifice of
a sky falling through the whole of itself, onto thin *Penitentes.*

IV

How to travel the face of our closest star. Observed
telescopically as dust on a lens. A scrap on a breadboard.
Latched onto hope as tentatively as a pinhead. Silhouetted,
dressed as Venus moving quietly in transition.

Tomorrow, I Will Take Care

In the dip before dreams
I repeat that tomorrow
can be loosened

Its incumbent chokehold
on roughening teeth
Peppered grey cheeks

Serum on edema
Release feet treacled in the
twist: maintain leanness

Sedentary positions are
unable to resist obscene
refrains

As each day rises like
a curdled sun
Say something to yourself

Gantries are prised away
As is time, as is excuse
Be a muscular derivative

Effortless distance runner,
to *'become'* is antithesis,
excessively realised

All of Me

There is translucency   in a body
The separate limbs and trunk   attached
to a soul
Wrapped in squid skin   transparent
Filled with memories
        Stacked within a library abandoned
                    or swallowed in the
briny cavern of   a whale
Where dust prevails over shelves as
scales cover fish
                    all liquidy and thin
Covers overlooked   Spines ignored
Flipping through ink and pulped pine
Titles cryptic like
            'This Wholesome Ghost'
'Nothing Human Left to Find'

Piled up   these books are organs
Stitched together hearts   eyes
and   lungs
                    The guts of it
Just human parts roughened and formed
into   shapes
Imperfect as life   Its uneven lines
Written like all of us   trying to tape
together pages

Gather   up   these   twisted   insides

Obligate Carnivore

Staring at clouds is escapeless, as in grey shapes dissipate. No ladders here to climb, time wasting away like employee of the year. Certificates pinned to bare chests, a stiff shirt buttoned back up, whilst someone asks about blood leaking from suburban yards. The self, haunted as a house. To walk inside mirrors as identical twins. Children fed milk soured by the sound of feet climbing up stairs. Yet still, gold is everything. A nagging intent. Future continuity as a jawbone breaks, then heals   breaks   *repeats history.* Hoisted up into navel trees, taut body, stiff roots, the rounded tears of fruit citrus thick with pith. Stones between fingers, its uneaten flesh. *Obligate carnivore,* bereft. Depleted of essential acids. Blue legs unpleasantly bruised. A reliance on cuspids, on reduction settling discreetly, as dust does, in the disparate homes of disparate men.

Assimilation

It takes a while to knead   to decimate, fit neatly between
pelvis or sternum

Where grown grass has gone to seed, and cloudforms
The light seen from the inside out   is *illusionary*

Until we are seamless   as skin, a leg bending back
an arm folding in

A sharing of blood and oxygen as if anticipating loss
The subsequent grief hung up   A well-worn suit

Until it's time   to untangle   pick out loose threads
No need to scoop out a body   live instead   as a monolith

Fulfill destiny   be *complete*

Without sharing space with lemon-tinged skies   its buzzing
backs ready to sting, or fleetingly,   block out the sun

Pelican at Night

My pelican is a night bird
His abject eyes are
anti-matter

He gulps me into the
pot of his stomach
My impression on the
sheet of his throat

He ingests my dreams
Coughs up a fishbone
Some starlight

And the day propped up
on the bottom of my heels
A daub of red paint or a
crucifix

So he might pause
alone at the footboard
His tentative bill
opening and closing with
a creak

Disappointed Moon Poem

Your rise & fall
of light, less heat

Asthmatic chest
squeezing dirt

Of time drawing
in its air

Axis calibration
The spoils of war

Crude oil on a
gulls wing

Of negligence or
endless tides

This sadness of
pale porcelain

Spins slowly
The hanging nail

hooked
on ruptured fear

To dying mothers
Father figures

unable to outwit
gravity's leash

Oh poor moon
Your seas

are showerless
Spilling tears

Its rocks & dust
trail ridges

Helpless as
an orbit

Your magnolia
cheeks

Comfort Food Instructional

Cookery requires adherence to lists. Reminders to remove fingers and thumbs cleanly, to *cleave*. Remove below wrists, sauté in oil. Fry evenly before swallowing. A taste of marrowbone. Its disguise is hollowness, is ubiquitous, an example of how to manipulate *papillae*, solidify proteins. Render crisp lean fat, de-bone and butterfly. Chargrill to blacken. An exact preparation of rack ribs. Remove lips, save the eyes. Deliciously sightless, such rich and sumptuous silence. I cook, I eat, I take the meat then sharpen, use specialist knives. Season and braise, tenderize, boil lightly. Rest then peel. Carve with precision, serve myself up, the *grandiose* of assembly. How avoidant my muscles, these spacious cavities. How very well practiced, for restauranteurs. For gastronomists who chew between teeth. These avoidance techniques acquired through various displeasures. *This solace to be found in comfort eating.*

On/Off

I tell myself that I'm dying. That despite the vomiting heat and cell division, I've failed. Drawing out the pinkness of thick mesoglea. Irukandji heart shrinking with sclerosis. Both of you are transparent and *still* I eat myself to death. How to ignore roots, ignore love. Low battery measurements and multiple devices for the weight of macronutrients. *Add it all up in the museum of your inaction.* My body hurts. A rudimental clicking sound of on and off. Did I mention that I'm dying? It's just that I don't seem to be able to lift a finger to help.

The Kill

The river where the man made us untuck our shirts is fenced off and full of trash. Beneath my legs, right angled, the phalanx is cramping. White roses are torn up and scentless in a heap. I've been to Europe, Beijing, Los Angeles. Ungrateful of me to think that there are more beautiful places. A more beautiful body to live in, more meaningful work. Not just numbers, not *just* the numbers, or some mad caricature blowing breath into jars for comparison. Because a career is the lack of depth felt between sunrise to sundown. So let me reward you then, with dialogue. The words made by old mouths for the new and obligated. As a forkful of the rarest meat, the *manliness* of a tomahawk steak. On how to hunt, to drown out feeling. Be a sinking stone arcing downwards to an open palm, an awful finger. I wish that I could tell you my name or who I am. That I'm stretched out. An old button accordion, a trophy kill.

My Life as an Arcwelder

I fixate on a toenail,   today, a
melanoma face   Sometimes, deep
melancholy

                        The rate of
exchange between   holster and knife

My life as an arc-welder   is to
spark   release bluebottles
swarming steel
As reflected faces   mime quietly
in the visors   of protective masks

A locust technician   mounts plague
Its reason   is to hold me in
place   A steady head   A steady
hand etching reason

                        Magnesium
brightness is mantra   is task

When loss is everywhere   loose
metal scraps   wire string
Then electrodes   in the season
of moths
                        Mottled wingtips
Magnolia backs

                        Somehow seem
more important   than everything

Quiet Boys Clean Their Plates

A corpse flower unfurls
in retrospect
Scented with the waft of
rotten years
All fattened and familiar

A linearity, but repeatable
Sick of these man shapes
carrying maggoty loads
around maggoty waists

We eat when there's dread
When ordinary things
are trussed up
Like Saturday liver
Mistrusted

My mother is dead to me
And still able to force down
forkfuls of fat into
my oesophagus

I eat when I'm full
At night and hidden
When I finger my paunch
Folding bread like a gag
Like all good boys should

Fear-List Reflection Toolkit

How vampires are mistaken by the light. A tree, split open and ringless, afraid of other trees. A parentless moon spinning as a shield. Self-fulfilling prophecy. Black magic, sleight of hand. Shark attacks, blood leeching into coral reefs. How to shapeshift ~ into a bear, a lion, a lamb. An outcast thrown into wild hawthorns. To wage war on the body through ritual indifference. Zero hauntings. An interdimensional nothingness. Murder guilt as a fraudulent transaction. Bad actors enjoying the iron richness of organ meat. The mannerisms of my father as a cloak embodied. Defeated by my mother's teeth sinking in right up to the hilt. A family of Ming vases; counterfeit, cracked. Unable to pick up steel, put it down again, grow. The beauty of the world or accusations of lack of vision. The things *necessary* for a happy life. Reckless drivers, the lilt of bruised fists. Career suicide, self-persuaded. The potential for poor fathering, for choking on lint. Late heartbeats. A seen sparrowhawk but not flamingo. The cruel dismemberment of the young, and me, without real use. A low-lit postcard enslaved and forgotten in the noose of a dead town. Submission as the eternal bent nail. Nighttime escapes into preventable coffins. Publicly unsolvable maths equations.

Petals

No-one can see inside our stomachs, or the ivy creeping at the cuffs.

A slow rope from the eyes. A knotted centre tied around mouths,   behind blue lips.

Where the wafer of our love degrades, dissolving southwards to the earth.

Its obnoxious leaves sit long in the throat.
Rose stems wrapped around legs, the histamines,   our fear of flower-heads.

The poison of *Solanaceae* opening every night. To be trampled by our own two feet.   Because the truth, when tested,

is found within the filament, the style. Its magnificence of colour,   the petals resting in the snare of a *wild loneliness.*

Or just morbidity.   The increasing frequency of cardiac arrest.

Grief Poem (Kæster Hákarl)

I cut the gill shape of
a shark on my finger.
My face, roughly shaven.

Inside the wound,
a lingering seabed silent as
the winter sun.

This lightless fermentation
for the drowned.
Tri-methylamine blood.

The fleshy remnants.
Looted memories of
motherless slow swimmers.

A hundred years submerged
and *still* this grief in the
drying shed.

An Eqalussuaq then.
Dragged away to some
inconsequential beheading.

Sex Ed.

When I came, you took my face and screwed it to the batten. Blew me up like bubblegum. Laughed as you dropped me between old bottles, unwashed. Knowing that repeated steps expedites the very loneliness so quick to learn. Flushed and found in knotted shoulders, the pubic hair, the imperfections of a bent spine pushing out a stomach. A boy obsessed with anxious measurement as you laughed our ending onto the page. My confused sex printed on the beige of a second-hand mattress, a single bed. Unaccustomed and without choice. The laugh along pornographers, the dimples in their cheeks. Tipping their hat to awkward nakedness. Her afternoon noises. His encouragement and the way I blinded in the warmth of their contempt. I still feel the sparseness of misled summers. The cracks between the old, closed curtains. The movements of their bodies, their missing heads.

Submission

The crow in my lap
is anti-particular.

The head in a box
perpendicular to mine.

And the afternoon,
an airless cloche.

Promises everything
but necessary flight.

Promises no answers
except procedural

routes that lead
to corvid. Warmth a

diminished return
for handcuffs.

To know roughly
that this is all there is.

Black feathers and
pearlescent tip.

Late Afternoon as a Metaphor for Entrapment

The window is open / *with the working* / with despair / with a sing song / with Aprils propaganda / with its warmth / false flags / unachievable summers / unfulfillable romance / my lifelessness in a swivel chair / and the innocent / with *no idea* about the working / the man with the washer / has *done* with the working / oblivious to death / obsessed / with the cleanliness of things / things working *just fine* / percutaneous biopsy of plastics punctured / bitten off by the working / the guilt of not spending every second with the working / flesh fuel for funeral cars / peeled from the working / slaves to the working / forgotten children's faces / washed by the working paternity leave for the working / loan payments for the working / beds readied for the working / folded *so neatly* by the working / the twenty-one grams of the working / their backs the greenstick spines of the working / as the glass spills the milk of the working / Magpies call from the branch / that held last year's leaves / *the working! / the working!* / the evening cars the voices of youth / so long in the distance / light is balanced on the edge / a singular orangeness of roe / and the window is open still / just slight enough / for it to set / like a guillotine welcoming night

Hunter / Gatherer

Know unenviable tradition / the sharpening of swords / a
gathering of pyramids / starches / sweet berries / Beauregard

Carve furrows hard fought / as steel blunts / our outgrown
clothes / in a town peeling away scales / wriggling free / from
the whole skin

When there's nothing else to do but eat / write out
prescriptions / for slow hearts and arms / the removal of clots

Beetroot purpling / pale palms

In four corners / *paint me in vanilla* / there is gratefulness in
pretence / that *all I am* / is relentless fate / something
predetermined

My nature cut out with scissors / that somehow / there is joy
in learning how to kill

Illuminated Refuge

The night is self-absorption.
  A wing gnawed open and quietly
alive. Eighteenth of the eighth

  two thousand and thirteen. The morning
she arrived. Through blackberry season,
  swans in winter. We reddened fingertips,

enjoyed slow swimming. Within her I hold
  these pieces of myself, yet this thoughtlessness
gathers under parasitic skies. Our birthdays

  become birthdays become birthdays,
 as she sleeps. An arm around my neck, a louse
  upon my face. This connection to the earth,

of time and space acerbic in the air. My
  daughter is all of me, *but not mine*.
For if I could live here completely in the wholeness

  of summer, as a good father, *a good man*, then I
would wrap myself in a doorway. This illuminated
  refuge of a fleeting halfway house.

IV.

New Year's Day

Increasing shades of morning swilled in
glass. Pinprick wounds, pewter hollows.

The crescent of silver thumbnails pushed
through skin, and torn, falling towards

the mantle of the body. A spinning globe
cracks its bones into thirsty soil, to sprout.

Grow arms and legs in silence all tangled
up and knotted in our thorn filled rooms.

From a distance an orange vice-gripped
in the jaws of a dog fills the air with pith.

Citrus misted on the fingertips of an out-
stretched hand glisters with its juice and

smacks across lips. A tang to draw out
the spit of dawn, a promise to the world.

As we float towards its heavy moon our
limp necks cradled, our too heavy heads.

Rebirth

A horse corpse folded at the bottom of the rocks spreads colour and warmth. The pillow grey sky scratches its scalp across crowns, the spears of treetop pines. Under the weight of ice, he belly crawls back to his god. A diamante bracelet bent clasp and scattered. Dirty sheets, stubborn cracked slats. Ribs slid between besides the bloat of unspeakable things pushed out. To expel the last breaths of life under cloth. A mountain Palomino closing its jaws around that to be born again, and after the passing of constellations, the frost unclenches its fist. To the rise of breath. To the sound of splitting spines. Emergent fingers, then arms, a face. Nakedness shaded white and innocence resting powder-like on the ground. And somehow the world is different. Not death or the carcass of *Equus* slipped from hidden edges. But goose gander skin, the exquisite lightness of feet rolling in the snow. Something lost then. Something trapped within the hazelnut of its dried open eyes.

Thumb / Forefinger

It's an orbitless question   A nothingness on
the tongue   In the hands, eggshell blue

Plutonic, somewhat igneous   Mining the
depths for truth, but   translucency

I have broad shoulders as instructed   My
lacrimal ducts   now older   still

produce tears   not heavy enough
to crack shells   Because fractures   Because fear

I'm supposed to be well rounded   Live happily
outside an eggless nest   My identity demands it

My gender   This acquiescence of calcium
a permeable barrier of   *would-be* compressive

strength, that side to side   between thumb and
finger   is   breakable   regardless

Splits yolks   That despite nausea can be
plucked out   Observed then, before discarding

Garden Variety

How to write about sadness, the folding of a towel? The horizon and its towers have disappeared today, soaking up towards the sky along with everything else.

The raw stump lopped off. Its sap, the yellowness dropping early to floors, to furnish. Do trees scream when tortured? or the frequencies of an empty house, its vacuum. How *large* everything is.

I've filled it with music, floated on the stairs. But there are two people competing for attention. I've fed them, dressed them in indifference.

One is older than the other and it shows, that despite introductions, there isn't much room. One set of limbs to push into, the other will be freed.

And I don't know where they'll go, but I'll walk the borders in the future tense. Pruning bushes, Gooseberries, Pippins. The garden varieties for all the years of dead light. Dead blossom on the end of bent fingers.

The First Time I Didn't Disappear

Grief is just winter thickening. Oatmeal around a spoon
stirred too long and aching in the hand. The way paper
from December gifts wilt upon the floor. Curling upwards, a
hardened skin. A yellow heel peering through a sock. Three
chairs pulled closely together and only the screech of legs to
halt silence. The walls he lived in plastered over. Hidden gold;
a smirk, a glint in the eye. The watching ghosts lurking, in part,
like flags flown at half-mast. And the kitchen, the heart of the
home, overcooked. In summer, blackened with thunderflies.
Blackened from the wood fire at Yuletide. Blackened from
the lies pushed into bags and stuffed. Only to be found after
death had passed, laughing in front of our faces as we tried to
tell good tales. Every time I sat and thought that I had loved,
I disappeared. The voice picked out. Stamped upon. Placed
amongst the turquoise chocolate of the nest eggs fallen from
the tree. And then the body, transmuted. With every church
bell an open mouth shrieking. Through the glass we'd see
the swallows start to ready. The summer bent around a pole,
the sourness of Swiss chard. Ants missing the fire of sun and
the grass wet with the choice of those able to swill it out and
around, to spit saliva in an arc. I am stolen every time my
back bends the fibers of this wicker seat. Until today. Now
there is an island and filigree and chrome. A sign that he has
gone. South maybe, to sit brining in the water butts. To stand
against the window to press his face. A shadow banished, left
alone.

Six Dead Bodies

The first, powder pinks, greys.
A directionless travel to nowhere
but gradual exhalation.

·

My father in his bed, glowing.
That he might leap up, a lightning bolt.
November blues, bad jokes.

·

Roadside Morocco; honeymooning.
Scarlet and mustard fabric, face down.
Absence marooned in dust.

·

Fluorescence clothed in paper.
Swan feather tiles, a spearmint shroud.
Questions about relief, about vessels.

·

A periscope, an oxygen tank within a
skull. Submariner filling flasks with air.
Breach ashen piles, rise up little boat.

Things are Beautiful Really

The lies I've told myself about
living are covered with a sheet
and embroidered

Pictures of a winter house
Lights hanging in a dry jaw of air
Our places of illumination

The moon a goblet of eternal
youth, and me, a liar,
slipping like a hand

Things are beautiful really
Her discarded shoes, the sky as
smalt

I'll lose the way it presses down
upon my body, and similar to
real families, my happy friends

I have the opportunity but lack the
effort. I'll speak to her and maybe
we can agree

On how best to colour things in
How to select the sharpest needles
for the thread

Candy Floss

Share a cloud then, knowing that red is the colour. Spin its sugar on a loom. That it is wet and stale as old bread sliced into gutters.

Hold onto me, this weather. The shipping forecasts, low pressure, the cold fronts and occlusions. That when split open spill sparks, silver, like knives fallen from a drawer.

And with sticky handfuls I lighten, knowing that all I want is pinned upon the blue sky. Reaching towards transcendence, *like a crow on the updraft*   I imagine.

Acceptance

becomes apparent in the tuning
of the wires. In the night-breath.

Along the scalp of a streetlamp
brightening the cold road below

When the complexities of the
moon can simply be described

as a pearl sewn above the sag of
last year's leaves, then it's here.

Like an eye lusting louder than
trivialities, too quickly closed.

And valueless things can be lost.
A box of items used and packed

away in memory to be respected
but not asking to be knelt upon.

Some moth-eaten clothes thrown
out and tentacled over the top.

A choice that always seems to sit
teetering on a blade's thin edge.

Of nervous energy and thought.
Half in, half out, of torn pockets

How to Fall With Grace

An apricot, the stone fruit
    swelling in our throats

Black as organs, a dull window
    The throb of missing teeth

Of shapes, the beetle-backs of
    cities all hollowed out

Its twilight apples like us alone
    Waspish on an orchard floor

The grass a cushion, a pillow
    To swallow silence like a nail

Sunk into, swallowed by the ground
    with the grace of a bone

A record of things once alive
    that can live again, in time

Twilight Ghost Meditation

My sails are velvet shorts. A white
boat sewn onto red seas where I call
out your name.

Gripped like plastic in the froth.
A long circumference three hundred
and sixty degrees across the weight of

oceans. Where eyes; sharp teeth, break
the surface for scraps and what might
be bitten off in time.

To be picked at. Serrated in a crewless
cabin, *O mysterious song,* your slab of
air fills a table.

The lazy rotten food, toothpicks flagged
with meat rocking backwards and
forwards with the tide.

The cutlery, its horizonless views are
endless. *What music!* dissected by the
chop, a rise and fall of triangles.

Some sloping squares or a white mouth.
How far can a boy drift before the rocks
draw him to a close, barrelled up on a

sword of sand to slip away. Swim now,
roll your hands ~ these windows expect
faces, young ghost. When you are

ready, *you will know*. Fingers drag the
air, the body floats, a spilled paint of
moon draped across its cloth.

Man Considers Climbing Out
Of His Body & Into Another

Though when we do this,
will they come for me?

Their claws, their quick hands.
A breathing in and out of walls.
To the land, a sowing of seeds.

My truth is
buried beneath the floor.

They fill the quiet places,
between pillows and sleep.
When a door clicks in the night.
When a child holds a finger gently
like a twig.

This lull behind my face,
This gap.
This lingering between.

They will knock you with a Gavel.
Ring the hood of your skull as the
upward fields grow green,
and the tree -

The tree outside is leaning in?
To listen?

To listen, feel.
To wrap roots around a
house heaving up its
skirt of earth to run away.
Dust in an attic space.
The spill of dreams through
gaps in a worn sash.
In sleep, hurt skin holds
the sound of trains.

(Gather pace then, tentative heart)

How would they come for me?
Pain in lieu of love?
Deep water to drown?

Deep and yes

How high will the crops grow?
How hard will it be to
harvest them?

Very tall.

Very hard to.

But I'm little and
afraid to fall.

Present beneath everything,
below it all.
A talk of thinness.
Of exhalations blowing
down bricks.

Little pig   Little pig

Please

Let me climb in

Acknowledgments

Sincere thanks to the editors of the following journals, where some of the poetry in this book first appeared: *Acropolis, Butcher's Dog, COMP: An Interdisciplinary Journal, Ice Floe Press, The Poets Directory,* and *Osmosis Press*.

Thanks also to the following for their support and inspiration; Aaron Kent & *Broken Sleep Books*, Jo Clement, Emily Brenchi, and Hannah Hodgson @ *Butcher's Dog Magazine*, Zoë Brigley, Seanín Hughes, Charlie Baylis, Jaydn DeWald and Piedmont University, Louise Mather & *Acropolis Journal*, Robert Frede Kenter & The Editorial Team at *Ice Floe Press*, Colin Bancroft & *Nine Pens Press*, Briony Hughes & *Osmosis Press*, Michelle Maloney King & *Beir Bua Press*, P.A Morbid and *The Black Light Engine Room Press*.

Thank you to my wife Caroline, my daughter Dorrie and my sister Amanda.

LAY OUT YOUR UNREST

Lightning Source UK Ltd.
Milton Keynes UK
UKHW040620141122
412164UK00001B/6

9 781915 079336